TOXIC

A Compilation of Short Stories, Uncompleted Novels, and Poems

Sarah Dill

ISBN 979-8-88751-903-6 (paperback)
ISBN 979-8-88751-904-3 (digital)

Christian Faith Publishing
832 Park Avenue
Meadville, PA 16335
www.christianfaithpublishing.com

Printed in the United States of America

Toxic

Why do I call this toxic?
Here's the thing
Toxic's for the readers like us—you and me
We're all toxic to an extent, and yes that's true
As much as we deny it but point it out in others too
We see their splinter but ignore our block
As we choose to ignore our own faults
There's a love for us
The purest of love
Even if you don't choose it
Emotions are a part of all of us
That's why I choose to write
Emotions are what I follow headfirst
Into this thing called life
For better or for worse
I write to relate
To all of our toxic traits
Some choose to grow
Others say no
Some of us blame the others who cause our trauma
Dontcha know
The good Lord gave me this, but I don't know why
So I write for him
And his glory by and by
I relate to the emotions
That we commonly have

The experiences that are way too often
Just a tad
It's toxic, you see
You and me
Even though no one wants to be
But I write to grow
And I write to show
The love I want others to know

Lonely

I'm tired and lonely
As you can see
The contact I want
Is either cut off or removed from me
I'm tired of the adult hissy fits I pitch
Because it creates more problems than I care to admit
The more I crave for some sort of contact
The more I push myself to be alone
I've taught myself from the start
That talking and rambling isn't that part
I can't help it you see, it's the perfected mosaic art for me
So behind a cheerful appearance and stories that last for miles
Is a little girl wanting to be held for a long, long while
Well, don't stand there and pity me
There's lots more to do before the day is done
Let's get up
Get going
Come on, let's go
Ignore the drama queen with words spilled all over the floor

Am I Okay with Just Okay?

Am I okay with just okay?
Is it rude or is it safe?
I don't even know the pace
I should be taking
Is it wrong or is it right?
There's no way this is black-and-white
But there just isn't time to put up a fight
Darling, I don't know what to say
But am I okay with just okay?
Put on a show
Be okay with how it goes
It's just how life rolls
You have no control over the actions of others
But if it's messed up, it'll be your fault for hours
Now watch your words and control what you say
No one wants to know if you've had a bad day
And if you do let them know,
Oh, what a disgrace!
Did you see your mother's disapproving face?
Am I okay with just okay?
I wanna let them in
Let them know how I feel
Okay, never mind
That's just unfair attention that I would steal

It's always based upon what you say
Am I okay with just okay?
Listen here
You're okay with just okay
No one cares like that, dear
Whether it's the right thing to say
You better be okay with just okay

Okay…

Smile Baby, Smile

Hey, why are you crying? Oh you're okay, just smile baby. There we go, better already!

What are you doing? I can't believe you're embarrassing me like this. You are five years old, quit your crying!

Oh what's wrong, baby? Well, are you a big kid? Big kids don't cry in public. There ya go, baby, just smile.

You're depressed? I don't believe that. I mean, you're so sunny and smiles all the time! Well, let me tell you about what happened to me.

What do you mean you're uncomfortable with him? You're always so friendly and welcoming. Just smile, baby, he'll get over it.

Smile!

Just smile, baby, it'll be all good!

When Life Feels Like

I like it when life feels like a baby's laugh, pure and innocent, with a hearty laugh at that. When happiness is so contagious, you can't help but join along. When it all fits together, it's a perfect sporadic little song. You see something simple in a funny light because they're truly experiencing it for the first time.

I like it when life feels like lightning bugs on a summer night. Sporadic flashes and an adrenaline rush, just trying to see who can catch the most bugs. When it's cool and calm and everything fits right into place, the chaotic running and screaming of children are somehow almost needed.

I like it when life feels like fishing. There's calm in the world, and everything is indifferent. You're with your loved ones, and the hours quickly fly by, but it was only moments ago you sat down side by side.

I like it when the world feels like spending time with a good friend. There's no judgment, and the stories never end. You're constantly full, and you feel at home, but you most likely need to leave because morning shifts come early. The space feels completely uninterrupted, and it all just fits, like you're not trying or turning into something you're not.

I like it when life feels like reading a good book. There are stories untold, and your attention is captured. The calm and cliff-hangers that held between each page. And the soft little nook you could read in for days. It's a whole 'nother world where there's no alarm unless you're reading a horror book, then yeah, good luck falling asleep.

I like it when life feels like the first time eating a brand-new dish. The flavors come together, and it creates an experience you'll want to revisit. It's new, and you can't help but be excited. And when the waiter comes with it, oh, you can't wait to try it.

I like it when life feels like a campfire. Yeah, I know the smoke is unpleasant, but there's something about sitting around a fire, feeling the warmth and the joy radiating off the people around you. There's a blissful peace among the smoke—the laughter, the jokes, and of course, the toasted marshmallows. Silly songs and lightning bugs glow. No one ever wishes to go home.

I like it when life feels like a fuzzy blanket and a cup of cocoa on a rainy eve. The peace of the air, the warmth of the blanket, and the consistent pitter-patter of raindrops against a glass pane. The cocoa warming you up with every sip and thinking it doesn't get better than this.

The War Is Coming

The war is coming
And it's scaring me
Can't they see how close we are to meeting thee?
The war is coming
I feel so alone
What happens when they destroy our home?
We know not the day
The hour
The time
But I know exactly
The good Lord is mine!
He's protected me since day one
This fight has already been won
The possibility of war scares me
Even though you're coming soon indeed
I still wonder of the possibilities

Be an Adult

What are you doing?
Quit crying
You're a mess!
And you wonder why I stress
Dust off the dirt
You'll be fine
Ugh, you try me every time!
From say "mama"
To "shush it, I'm on the phone"
To "why don't you talk to me anymore?"
From "come on, say dad"
To "you're not doing that right"
But, Dad, it's only my first try
To "I'm the man of this house. No questions asked. That's why"
And finally "sit down and do as you're told"
Be grown
Express your feelings
Not the negative ones, of course
Pick your jaw up off the floor
Tell us how you feel
Now don't say a word
Why do you ignore us, we're quite hurt
Being an adult is what we dreamed
That is until right about 17
The stress increases
The elders get worse
And they're confused on why we're not at church
Let us in with a warm love
Don't give us time to think

"What are they thinking of?"
Give us the strict you were raised on
But please don't let us be scared of you causing us harm
We know you try
Believe us we do
But don't shut us out when we wanna discuss
The faults and issues
As adults should
We've felt what we've felt
We've seen what we've seen
Please don't dismiss us
It's no different from when you were 17
Oh, shush
Be an adult
I don't know what you're mentioning of

A Time like This

Hey
I don't mean to be such a disappointment and a pest
I'm sorry, I'm having a moment, I must confess
I see all the people in your world
And I wonder why
Why can't I be like that
But do I even try
I go for a day
Then the devil hits my heart
I cry as I wonder how I've gotten this far
Lord, I don't see a reason for my existence
You do, for whatever reason
I really wanna take care of your people
Love and feed them
Care and make them feel needed
But there're so many people who'd execute my plans better
And get them out to the world
As if they're as light as a feather
As I lay and roll around in my fears
A gentle voice I hear
You were made for a time like this
I'm sorry, have you seen this mess
They're crazy, and they'll continue to walk over me
You know they'll do my talents better
Please
My child, I love you
I haven't gone away
I put you here
You'll find out why one day

You're made for a time such as this
With a sassy mouth and quick wit
The heart you have
I made for sure
Those passions you have
Let them burn and roar
The times you come to learn of me
Are the ones I cherish indeed
You're made for a time like this
You'll soon see
I made the world in 6 days
Isn't that true
I knew there was a need for someone like you
You're made for a time like this
And don't forget
I'm here always
Even if you feel like I've already left

Wait

I know waiting is the goal
But it's frustrating
I wanna be the one dictating
I know waiting helps us grow
But my childish self wants to stomp and shout
No, no, no!
I want it now
I want it my way!
I don't understand why you're making me wait
Hey, Lord, that hurt
I'll make it your fault!
It's easier to lock a bat in a vault
What we want in minutes seems to last days
No wonder none of us like to wait
The time we wait is the time to prepare
So we must pray and learn until we get there
Because that might be the only time we have spare
Life is up and at 'em
Let's go, go, go!
Now hold on
Take a minute
Just be easy
Notice how God made today's air nice and breezy
Clouds perfectly flutter a bluebell sky

And the sun covers everything far and wide
Now what else will his creation hold
For that, we do not know
And while we could create possibilities for days
Honestly, my darling
Let's just sit here
And wait

There's Just Something about a Hug

Physical touch is a weird thing. It's some people's love language, and others are perfectly fine not having ever to feel it again. It's a touchy subject in today's world (no pun intended), and as everyone should, consent is heavily relied on. People have misused, abused, and greatly twisted the actions of physical touch.

But there's just something about a hug.

From personal experience, I am very picky about who receives a high five or a fist bump as well as hugs. I know many people are, and that's okay. As soon as I give a hug or receive one, I'm the last one to let go. I can't help it. There's just something about a hug.

The simple comfort it gives and how calm you feel afterward. How does one hug speak a thousand words? There are people who can put stitches on torn hearts with their hugs. Those with the one-arm hugs make you feel special because you know they rarely give those out. The ones that are given out constantly but you still accept simply because of how much care is put into it.

As a child, you feel safe and secure, wrapped in a parent's arms, where nothing can go wrong. As an adult, we get busy and on the go to the point when someone asks us, pent-up tears wiggle their way out. Come on, there's just something about a hug.

Safety

Sadly, comfort is a hard thing to find. People abuse it, misuse it, and find it in the wrong places. The most genuine place to find it is within our own homes, yet way too many call it our war zones.

Home

Your hugs feel like home.
Your voice is my safe place.
I trust in the Lord, but you're my next best thing.
You have no idea how I view you and all that you do.
My home shouldn't be a human, but weirdly it's true.
People are temporary, something I know to be true.
It's occurred over and over until I thought, what else is new?
While I wait for that to happen too, I feel safe, why's that something
     I've never known?
The best people say that you're stronger when a person isn't your
     home, but I can't help that you're my safe escape.

God Bless the Broken Road

A bit of a previous attempted novel

"Class, class, settle down. Now go get ready for the ballet lesson," Mrs. Leonard said as she brushed by the mirrors with a stack of papers in her hands. Faith walked beside me as we dragged our tote bags with us.

"Oh, this is a chance of a lifetime! I may have a chance to dance with Heath Smith!" she gushed, pulling out her leotard and tights once we came to the girls' locker room.

"Calm down. First, you don't have to say his full name every time." I went into the stall to change. They didn't need to see my reminder of last night. "Besides, you have a chance to dance with him in this class till the end of the semester."

I came out of the stall with my long-sleeved black leotard and a pair of black sweatpants. We followed the other girls to the dance room while Faith was trying to argue her point about Heath.

"All right, class, your partners are on the list on the mirrors. Find them, choose a room, and begin after you pick up your music." Mrs. Leonard swished away after instructions.

People rushed to see the board, girls crossing their fingers for Heath and the guys hoping for Alice. I finally worked my way through after seeing Faith trying to hide her slight disappointment because she was working with Zeke instead of Heath. I ran my finger down the list, halting when I saw my name.

A finger accompanied mine, and a hand started to rest lightly on my hip. I jerked away to see the one and only Heath looking at me.

He looked back at the list and whispered to me, "Well, I guess we'll be dancing together this week."

I looked back to see what he meant.

No, he can't be right. This can't be happening. I stared in wonder at how this could be possible.

"You ready, Kasei?" he asked, holding out our music.

I took the music and followed him into room 2. He held the door open like a gentleman would do, but all I could hear were my father's and boyfriend's words ringing across my mind.

"Gentlemen only exist for the pretty girls. You're lucky I took a look at a trash bag like you."

"You ready?" Heath's voice broke my thoughts.

"Huh? Oh yes, I guess."

He leaned around me to press Play on the computer. My head was overrun by anxiety, but in the midst of it all, a voice broke through—a small still voice.

"Trust me."

"Heath, did you say something?"

"No, but Kasei, are you sure you put the disk in?"

"Oh, it's still in my hand. Here." I handed him the disk, curious about who said something.

"Trust me, Kasei. Trust Heath."

Heath turned around and held his hand out, "Are you ready?"

I couldn't speak. I just slipped my hand into his. The first few beats started, and he led me closer to the mirrors. I looked down at my feet to reposition myself, only to have my face tilted upward.

"Just let go," mumbled his deep voice. As if involuntarily, I followed his command. The music flew around us, guiding us into leaps and turns.

I spun away from him as he stood by himself on one side of the room. He ran toward me after I froze in a position with my back to him. His large hands picked me up by the hips, and he rested the small of my back on his shoulder. I drew one leg into my stomach as the other turned into a stiff board as he turned toward the center of the studio.

Heath set me down and turned me to face him. He made a lunge toward me as I leaned away. I was caught off guard when his hands returned to my hips and lifted me into the air with a spin. He slid me down himself and leaned his face toward mine, our noses touching.

Why is he this close? I stared into his dark gray eyes.

"Kasei…," he breathed, sounding as if he was on his last breath.

"Ms. Williams."

The sound of Mrs. Leonard's brisk voice caused me to jump away from Heath.

"Mr. Smith, while I do enjoy both of your techniques, that is not the method of dance I told you to go over, is it?"

"No, ma'am," we both responded. I hid my head in embarrassment, trying to hide the probably glowing red face I had.

Mrs. Leonard directed her voice toward me, "Ms. Williams, I hope to see you after school to go over today's lesson properly."

"Yes, ma'am."

"That goes for you too, Mr. Smith. Do you understand?"

"Yes, ma'am."

He sounded defeated, but when I tried to look at his face, he had turned away. Mrs. Leonard's voice rang out, telling everyone to go to the showers.

"Heath," I whispered, not knowing what to do.

His head barely turned my way when he said, "You danced really well today. See ya tonight." Heath grabbed the stuff and slipped out of the room.

Truth

Lord, I didn't get the answer I wanted in our prayer time today. I wanted to just sit there and complain. It's one of the easiest things to do. I wanted to tell you how my mind runs away with the smallest of actions and how everything appears the way it's not. It's like everything gets tangled in giant knots. I wanted to tell you about how I wasn't satisfied with myself and what I did that day.

I wanted to tell you that I'm a waste of space, and there are so many other people who can accomplish all I want to in life so much better. With the talents that I have, someone else can do better.

Lord, I tried telling you that. And you know what happened?

Before I could even say anymore or even try to convince you that I was right, you asked me this:

Do I know your truth or my truth?

To tell you the truth, I didn't like that question, not one bit, because it made me recognize that I was trying to tell the living God how my path was going to go. The God who breathed new life into me knew exactly how I was and every little detail of my existence.

I tried telling you how it was going to be. You're a patient God, and that's more than I've ever deserved. You understand the struggle I face, and you're here with me. I know I've hurt you, and you still let your son die on the cross for me.

There's so much truth in the Bible if I just read it, yet I think of when I have those weak moments the devil knows he can poke and pester with. Sadly, he picks and picks at it, knowing I'll feel defeated.

My truth is a weird, twisted sort of thing. It reminds me of a fickle fruit vine. The berries and the bright green leaves are the moments where I recognize my best.

"I'm one of a kind."

"I have a sweet and caring heart."

"I'm blunt, feisty, and sassy—what a beautiful combination."

It's the moments where I don't hate the mirror and see your beautiful creation, which you deserve complete credit for.

Now the majority of the time, I see the twisted, dull, dry, thorny vines that largely cover my vision.

"You're so fat—look at that double chin. And oof, you need to wax."

"I can't believe you just keep talking. Are you really that desperate for someone to see you?"

"You're so slow. How do you even have a job? They all can work circles around you. No wonder no one wants you in a management position."

"How did you gain that much weight? Gosh, just stop eating."

I think of the harmful, twisted, and sharp words to cut deep, to whip myself into the person I want to be. That's my truth, and the truth I now see is completely false. It's one of the worst opinions I've ever had. It's only ever scarred and cut me and left me so broken that I couldn't work to start on a better person.

Your truth, however, your truth is the one I should have had as my internal dialogue all along.

You said I'm loved.

You said I'm fearfully and wonderfully made.

You made me out of thy own image. You made me exactly as I should be.

You made me, knowing what was on my path, and you chose me. You would leave your ninety-nine sheep to recollect my lost self.

You have such an overwhelming, never-ending, reckless love for me.

I am the daughter of a king!

You created me from the start, and you made something beautiful.

So, Lord, yeah, you know your truth, and there's no truth like it.

You

You
You drive me absolutely insane
I can't figure out your words or your actions
Do you even know what's happened?
You are so self-centered and unaware
Of how many people you've put in despair
You whine and complain
Of things not going your way
That it's not fast enough
You're all alone
No one apparently loves you
And your house doesn't feel like a home
I'm sorry you've faced the emotions you've faced
But do you really think that it's only your fate
To cry out in pain
But brush everyone else away
Wake up
Look in the mirror
Why can't you see
That this is both you and me

With the Heart of a Lion

An uncompleted segment from a novel

Wood crackled around me, and flaming embers dug into my raw skin. I clawed at each ash, causing more harm than good. Coughing tore up my worn-out voice, yet I chose to call out into the blinding smoke once more.

"H-help," inhaling more smoke than my lungs could bear, "someone, please, anybody!" I kept stumbling forward, snapping my head upward toward a loud pop. Wood shards showered above me as the beams popped into pieces. Strong arms pulled my waist backward, and I screamed.

"Shhh, honey, it's me. It's just me." His voice comforted my shot nerves, and I spun around, flinging my arms around his neck.

My hands automatically gripped his soft hair, now singed from the heat.

"Where's your gear?" I pulled back as he pushed my frizzled hair away from my face.

"We don't have time for that. Let's go." He pulled me along, and I tumbled to the ground. Hunter huffed, and in one swift motion, I was being carried through the burning house.

"I'm sorry," I mumbled as he dodged crumbling walls and roaring flames.

"Let's just get out of here." He held me tighter as we made our way to the open door. Black smoke billowed around us in the crisp, bitter air, and the walls around us crackled from the heat.

The beams popped into pieces, and I shrieked. Hunter ran faster toward the door, and the house began to crumble fast around us.

"Hunter," I whined, wrapping my arms tighter around him.

He paused, looked up, and back to me. The door was just a mere few feet away from us, and he bolted for it.

It all blurred together—the smoke, the heat, and the sudden clear air. The brisk cold surrounded me.

His arms. They weren't there. I frantically looked around me, not finding him.

Heavy feet stormed by me, and the once-open door was blocked by flaming wood.

"Hunter?" I called out in disbelief.

"Hunter!"

What Would It Be Like

What would it be like for you
If I woke up and couldn't remember you?
While it is a scary thought indeed
I still wonder what it would be
Would it hurt when you first hear
That I didn't remember when I held you dear?
Would you bother to return our page
Or just let me not reminisce our days?
Would you be scared out of your wits
And go into a sobbing fit?
Would you pray, scream, or cry
As our moments slipped on by?
I'd hope you'd spend hours sitting with me
Telling how we used to be
Our talks, our stories, our random tales.
How we met and the things that failed
Would you get frustrated if I drew blank
When you said an inside joke or name?
When a day was mentioned and I got an event right
Would you be soaring sky-high?
I hope this never happens, I really do
But I'd try to do the same for you
What if I couldn't remember at all
Would that cause your heart to fall?
While this scary thing has happened to a few
I still wonder
What would you do if I woke up and couldn't remember you?

Bitter

There you go again
Consuming my mind
Controlling my thoughts
And yet I just let you
I think of the past, but the past is gone
But you're stuck in my head like a catchy song
You're addicting when you're not here
But it's probably good that we disappeared
I could admit that you're a mistake and move on
But I just don't wanna be wrong
I've hurt others, and now I guess it's time to hurt myself
It's not like I have much wealth
I see a future, but is it supposed to be mine
It's not like it's the right time
I struggle, but who have I made struggle more
Would it be better to drop dead on the floor?
I can't help it, I decided I couldn't wait
Now I guess it's my price to pay
I wanna go home, and no, not here
I'd rather you just let me disappear
It doesn't hurt, it just seems quite numb
But it all comes from being dumb
I need to learn a lesson, but I say I don't have the time
All I care about is a permanent mine
I hope you're alive, I hope you're okay
But what voice do I have a say
'Cause the voice that wishes you well
Is the one that hurt you beyond my simple understanding
Should I even be left standing?

Probably so, but here I am
Alive, well, but nowhere near a clam
You probably wish I was dead as I wish I was
It's funny how one thought turns into two
And I'm left in my own blue
I don't know how to help it
It's just easier to depressed of it
You're gone, but you never left
Can you just get out of my head
But no, it's always my fault
I couldn't be left alone for long

Easy?

From the beginning
Actually, the earliest parts
I knew that none of this would be easy by far
Your calling is true
Your name, I'll stand by
But what happens when the world catches my eyes
You've said before that both aren't an option
And the world, there are clearly some faults in
But it catches our eyes
Like a shiny little thing
And we're like a raccoon
Grabbing all we see
Following you is not said to be easy
That I know is true
But easy isn't what I'm here for
I'm simply here for you

Honeysuckle

You're like honeysuckle
Sweet. Short. Temporary
I ruin a lot just trying to fill that void
A little more sweetness, just a little more time
We all know you couldn't have been mine

Honeysuckle is a small treat
I guess that's why I always want it on repeat
A drop of honey is like a moment in time
I can't get it back, but I can be glad it was mine

Fallen Angel

You know the devil doesn't bargain
His beauty hides the dark pain he holds
You see the version he gives you
And when the red flags appear
They disappear as smooth kisses unfold
He plays with your sight
It's the quickest way to your mind
Your heart's already fallen
The devil doesn't bargain
He lies about his ways
He gets you with fear
And a fake love in his eyes
You long for his care
And the hurt makes you feel secure
Like it'll eventually turn into a home
The one you've been dreaming about
But don't you see
Being near him, and you still feel alone
He enjoys the loyalty as he betrays you each time
His grip gets tighter as more love lights up your eyes
The devil doesn't bargain
He plays off your wants
And you cave thinking it's your needs
Gentle touches are so much different than the rough way you know
Baby, there's a much better home
The devil doesn't bargain
People do change, but you have to know your boundaries as well
I hope you don't sit and dwell
It's hard when all you want
Is the fallen angel to bargain

Motivation Is Hard

Motivation is weird.

Some days, it feels like powering through five loads of laundry, cleaning the bombshell of a bedroom, making the best meal your family and friends have ever tasted, writing the world's best-selling novel, and accomplishing all your lifelong goals and dreams within five to twenty-five minutes.

On other days, it feels like wrapping yourself in a fluffy blanket, putting on fuzzy socks, putting on a playlist, or even just one song on full blast just to block out any thoughts or people for the day. Thanks to life, though, we can't just sadly put on pause and unwind during times of high stress and anxiety. But honestly, I am proud of you—yes, you. The one reading this, you've already powered through so much, socially, physically, emotionally, spiritually, and personally.

The Lord and yourself recognize what all you've been through, and even on the days you feel lower than the concrete under the carpet, you've constantly kept motivation. It may not feel like it, but you're here, clothed, and you've eaten today, hopefully.

But no matter how today turns out, Jesus and I love you so much, and we're so proud of you. I hope you know that even if I've never experienced the emotions you're experiencing at the level you're experiencing them, just know that I'll understand and be there with you. So will someone else, even though it doesn't feel like it.

Sending you some hugs, my darling!

Love Is. . .

An old coworker of mine made the joke of love is… Sarah Dill after I made a comment about drawers.

Well, it got me thinking of those comics from when I was a kid, and we'd get the *funny paper* (the comics) section of the newspaper. There was a spot down toward the bottom that would be titled *Love is…* and it would show something small.

Well, honestly, love can never be truly and fully explained until you experience it personally.

Love is complicated.
Love is simple.
Love is oblivious.
Love is discreet.
Love is bold.
Love is awkward.
Love is funny.
Love is sad.
Love is absolutely and utterly feeling insane.
Love is peace of mind.
Love is the gospel.
Love is a source of calm.
Love is blind.
Love is unknown.
Love is heavily felt.
Love is a glass of orange juice.
Love is the gift you've been wanting but can't afford.

Love is a hug.
Love is an "I'm so proud of you."
Love is running errands together in a sweatshirt and baggy pants.
Love is running out to get food when you both don't wanna leave
    the bed.
Love is a phone call.
Love is getting all dressed up.
Love is more than a label.
Love is an example of Jesus.

You see, love is so simple and beautiful and complicated to explain. So that's why, my dear, feelings and trusting your gut are the best ways to know your type of love.

When I Think of You. . .

When I think of you, I think of high hopes and big dreams. I think of big eyes that soaked up the world in wonder and awe of everything magical and beautiful. I think of kind words from adults and weird, awkward habits that small you had. I think of silly games, TV shows, and an imagination that could stretch farther than the Jordan River. I think of the world you lived in and wonder why you created it that way.

When I think of you, I think of a first memorable friendship. I think of the times I just wanted to hang out with you because I had a best friend. Finally, the ones that Disney told me would last me until I was old on a porch swing, and we'd sit there laughing at our crazy childish selves and all the people surrounding us at a young age. When I think of you, I think of not realizing how much I fought for your approval because, constantly, our friendship was on the line if I didn't do as you wanted. I think of the little girl who followed you around like a lost puppy dog because I lacked any other form of friendship at such a young age. I think of how much you've changed best friends over the years as I remember at an early grade I was the backup bestie.

When I think of you, I think of when reality hit. I think of realizing that school wasn't a happy place, that people tried getting to know you as a way of hurting you, and you weren't allowed to enjoy cartoons anymore. I think of her and wonder why she was always alone. Why she was the weird kid and why her originality was fuel for their laughs.

When I think of you, I think of a first crush. How I felt experiencing liking someone for the first time. I think of overreacting to each emotion and not realizing how to take it back a step. When I think of you, I think of the cookie-cutter perfect southern trophy prize. I think of the needed but unsaid apologies.

When I think of you, I think of finding something I have been around my whole life. I think of how I was taken out of my comfort zone and how beautiful unplanned situations are. Because when I don't see it written in my plans, I look back and discover how it was a part of God's plan. I think of the starting stones of a new relationship with you. I think of the wakening I truly needed and how my real life started to unfold. I think of the worry and concern that started us off, but it's being slowly replaced with trust and faith later on down the road. I think of the me I'm still working on now and how truly thankful I am that you haven't given up on me yet. Many would have left me behind because of my insecurities, scars, shortcomings, and faults, but you still hold my hand and say, "Come along, my child. I am with you."

When I think of you, I think of the crazed stage. I think of the hours of emotional drainage that were self-inflicted. I think of all the worries, stress, and pain I caused because I felt like I was behind on an imaginary deadline. I think of a little girl longing for something she didn't know how to give herself. I think of the start of a risky, self-centered stage. When I think of you, I think of one of the multiple reality checks I would receive.

When I think of you, I think of a black F-150. I think of truly falling for you. I think of believing your words and ignoring better judgment. I think of truly wanting to be in your life. I think of the fear of disappointing you. I think of how scared I was of you and how scared I still am. When I think of you, I think of me asking how high when you say I should jump. I think of everything being on your terms. I shake my head at myself for sneaking out because that was the hour you chose that you wanted my company. I think of my excuses and how my schedule wanted to revolve around you. How crazy I was. How it's still in me to have the gut feeling of what week I should check my phone for a call and when I should avoid certain foods. When I think of you, I think of still checking for your truck when I'm driving, just to see if I should watch my step. When I think of you, I look in the mirror and see desperate.

When I think of you, I think of kind eyes and a gentle heart. I think of when I first met the Lord; you were there. How your love for God shines brighter than anytime you've smiled. I think of texting for true guidance, wondering if it was a secret, selfish ploy for your attention. When I think of you, I think of loyalty and being genuine. How you greatly touch everyone you're around. How they love your presence. I think of how you're a true servant of God and how much you earn to learn more. When I think of you, I think of attempted apologies. I think of watching you grow in God's presence and how he has so much in store for you. When I think of you, I think of Psalm 23.

When I think of you, I think of sunflowers and gray buffalo plaid. I think of good times and true friendship. When I think of you, I think of selfishness and hurt. I think of how you felt the need to have it constantly in your control. How I tried to please you by doing everything you said. Truly, my darling, from my perspective, you've never been happy with yourself. While I can sit here and judge you, Matthew 7:1–2 said that I need to work on that, and you taught me a lesson I just now got and I wish to share it with you. Thank you for teaching me that if I don't learn to be happy with my situation now and I keep looking for the next big step that I want to be handed to me right now, I will never learn to truly grow and appreciate it when it arrives. And if I rush it, why, I just sour the experience, don't I? While I do long for the old friendship we had, where you saw a growing part of me no one else would have understood, it doesn't happen at the snap of a finger like you wished previously. When I think of you, I think of *why you're always in a mood.*

When I think of you, I think of the fact that I should probably be nicer to you. I try my best, but I never know how to communicate what I need from you. When I think of you, I think of copy and paste, and there's me! I think of trying so hard to prove I'm an original person and wondering what words that come out of my mouth are going to hurt your feelings. I'm thankful for you because you know and you try to understand. When I think of you, I think of coffee mugs, Jesus, and the big ideas you hardly tell anyone. I think of a selfless soul who's adored by many. I think of corny jokes and written devotionals. When I think of you, I think of how far you've gotten without killing me. I'm just kidding, Momma. When I think of you, I think of Piglet and determination.

When I think of you, I think of determination. I think of your strong will and great love for those around you. I think of how much you've been there and have loved me through it. When I think of you, I think of simplicity. I think of oversized sweaters and knee-high socks. I think of calling you *mom* before you were ever a *mom*. I think of a gentle and tough love when I think of you. So when I think of you, I think of Pooh Bear.

When I think of you, I think of someone who claims they're trying, but their actions always fail. I think of someone who needs to work on being a better friend. I think of someone who tries to pour out so much love that they leave themselves bone dry. When I think of you, I think of dogs and singing and learning the path God made for you. I think of the people who I didn't write about in this and how you're trying to include them without their feelings hurt. When I think of you, I see me.

Getaway

Sunlight beamed through the thin curtains as we curled further into the warm blankets. My eyes fluttered open to see your sleeping face. Peaceful and relaxed, not having a worry written on your skin. I slipped from under the covers and your arms and tiptoed into the kitchen to make your morning coffee. Outside, the world was at peace in the early morning hours. The dew was still perched quietly on the lively grass, and birds sang to the rising sun.

Two arms wrapped around my waist, causing my oversized T-shirt to rise up a little, and a head nuzzled sleepily into my neck. A sleep-coated voice mumbled into my neck.

"Huh?" I turned my head to see a messed-up bedhead burying itself into my shoulder.

"Come back to bed. It's cold."

I giggled and turned around in your arms.

"Baby, it's time to start the day. I've got your coffee brewing."

You whined and pulled me closer. "It's too damn early. Let's go back to bed."

"Come on now, look how pretty it is outside." I turned back to the window, and I felt your chin prop itself on my shoulder.

"It is pretty."

We both stood in silence for a few minutes as the coffee brewed and the sun rose higher in the sky.

"Thank you," you said softly, pressing a light kiss to my cheek.

"For what?"

"For the weekend escape. I needed it."

I turned to see your eyes looking back into mine.

"You're welcome. Honestly, everyone needs one, but right now, I can only afford yours and mine." I grinned ear to ear, and you laughed.

"You're a mess."

"Yes, but I'm the best kind of mess," I pointed out.

You looked at me in amusement and confusion. "And how's that?" you questioned, turning me to face you.

"'Cause you don't have to clean me up. All my messed up, colorful, jagged, soft pieces create this unique masterpiece called myself. You can just sit and watch as I strike a colorful picture into your life." I smiled up at you as you looked at me thoughtfully.

After a few, you wrapped the arm around my waist a little tighter and slipped a hand onto my cheek. Your eyes held so many wonders to them, and all they were doing was simply looking back into mine.

"And that's one masterpiece I don't mind spending all day looking at." You smiled as your lips lowered to mine.

I Can't Breathe

I can't breathe.

I can't breathe as I watch you. All you're doing is existing in your world, but it still stops my breath.

You've seen me, but you never looked.

Her eyes are locked on you. Smiling that smile, playing the cards they use to get the guy in the movie.

Even though Hollywood's fake, her moves are getting her the main prize.

You.

You never know what I thought, what I felt, what I did for you.

Maybe it's better to keep it that way.

They tell me to let it go if I'm feeling the way I do, but I want you protected.

Safe.

To know that you have a source of love, even if it's not the one I think I want.

I can't make people like me, they'd never be happy if I did.

My mind runs wild with the endless words and scenarios.

And it's killing me, but all I want is to see your smiling, happy self.

But now I see the truth, and I cannot help but die inside.

People you love should be happy, but how do you be happy?

I don't think you do, to be honest

I can't breathe.

I can't breathe as you wrap around her and glance back to me.

Giving her the attention she wants and the one I've craved ever since my immaturity existed.

Whether you know what I've thought is up in the air as your smile doesn't seem to fade when your eyes catch mine.

Your lips get closer to hers.

Closer.
And closer.
And even closer.
I can't breathe.
I can't breathe, I can't breathe, I can't breathe.
Looking away is my best option for my destroyed heart, but I can't.
There are times I've seen myself in her position, but who would've
    been in mine?
I can't breathe.
Slipping away, I managed to let a few tears slip before reality
    demanded me to get going on with life.
The walls get closer.
Your face flashes in my mind over and over.
Why are the walls getting closer? They don't move.
Your smile. Your sweet words.
I can't brush the walls away. I wish I could. They're crushing me.
Your beautiful eyes.
I'm being smothered in an open room.
A scream slices the walls around me, but they won't move. Another
    scream rips through my throat.
I can't breathe.
I can't breathe, I can't breathe, I can't breathe.
It doesn't help that you're the first to run to protect me from some-
    thing that only time can fix.
Your eyes are drowning in worry, and the walls are now on my lungs.
I can't hear you, but I see the words "what's wrong" slip continuously
    off your lips.
I can't breathe.
I can't breathe, I can't breathe, I can't breathe.

Control

You've let go of the future and put a death grip on the past. We'll just sit back and see how this goes.

Rocky

You chase after old and terrible choices
Not because you miss them
In a way you do
But you chase those because you're scared of rebuilding the parts of
your foundation that need fixing

I Love You

I love you.

I heard that phrase so many times from fans, dying for my attention as if it was their life fuel. Hey, it was all part of the singer's lifestyle, and I wouldn't change it for the world.

But I hadn't realized how many different versions there were until those three little words left his lips.

It's not like the situation prompted him to say it. We were driving over to my place after he picked me up from the airport. I was excruciatingly tired, and he was sweet enough to drive. We had the radio blasting, and we were yelling every lyric to every song on the radio. It was like every typical drive, just screaming songs, arguing over directions, and me begging for food.

"I'm so hungry!" I whined as we pulled into a gas station.

"Just give me a minute. I'll grab snacks. Or I could order pizza when we get to your place?" he suggested as he got out of the car, leaning in to see me.

"Is both an option?" I tilted my head, and he chuckled.

"Don't you judge my hunger!" I yelled as he slammed the door.

I watched him head to the station to pay for the gas, and I got out to pump for him.

As soon as I had finished and returned the pump, he walked out with a couple of bags and two slushies.

"I have the goodies!" He held up the bags as he reached the car.

"Yay!" I squealed like a little kid and ran toward my door.

Soon we were on the road, and I was digging through the bag.

"We have Whoppers, SweeTarts Ropes, three bags of Combos—um, yummy—Slim Jim, that's definitely yours," I said, pulling out what was mine.

"Share the Whoppers with me now." He laughed "Oh, and your Cherry Coke and Pringles are in the other bag. Don't eat all the Combos."

I gasped and rummaged through the bag on the console, squealing when I realized they were my favorite kind. I ripped the packaging open. I repeated *thank you* as I grabbed a stack of chips.

He shook his head at me, stealing glances at my childish state. I looked over to see the silliest grin on his face.

"What?" I mumbled with a mouth full of chips.

"Nothing." He smirked, and curiosity took over.

"Nuh-uh. You're always quiet when you have something on your mind. What is it?" I questioned. "Tell me!" I started poking him.

"Hey, quit it! We're gonna crash!" He swatted my hands, trying to keep his eyes on the road.

"Nope." I popped the *p* and continued.

He jerked the wheel, and I screamed at him to stop. He just laughed and continued driving normally. The ride was quiet except for the rattling of the snack bags and random burps. Stars flew around us, and the moon captured every shadow we saw. I leaned my head against the window and hummed one of my songs.

"Golly, I love you."

My head snapped up toward him. He was facing the road, but he seemed different. I never expected him to say that, not the way he meant. He seemed different, but it was comforting at the same time.

It wasn't like the comforting familiarity of a family member or a good friend telling you they love you. It wasn't anything like a first *I love you*—it wasn't that unfamiliar.

It sure wasn't like how my fans were screaming it from the crowds at every performance. It felt exciting but safe. Unusual but reassuring. It felt like he had said it a thousand times over, but he had only said it now. His eyes were caring and loving beyond anything I knew.

He looked over, and his smile fell. "Are you good? I'm sorry if I made you uncomfortable."

I brushed off his words. "Yeah, I'm okay. Just shocked."

He sighed and reached for his slushy. "I don't mean to make you uncomfortable ever. You know that."

"I know. I'm just unsure, ya know?" I fiddled with my fingers, shyly looking up at him.

He had a soft smile on his lips and understanding written in his eyes. He reached over and gave my hand a gentle squeeze.

"I get that. And I will try my best to respect that." He handed me the rest of the Whoppers, and the rest of the drive was silent. Although mixed emotions were in the air, it didn't feel awkward.

Picnic

Bright sunlight seeped through the blinds and past my eyelids. A groan escaped my lips, and I threw the blanket over my head. I tried returning to an uneventful slumber, but the harsh vibrations on my nightstand disagreed.

"Hello?" I groggily answered the phone.

"Well, don't you sound like sunshine and lollipops!" Eli's chipper voice rang through the phone, and it was a little much for this early.

"Eli, I just woke up. It's only"—I paused to look at the illuminated numbers on the clock—"it's 8:54? In the morning?"

"Exactly! Which means you've almost slept the day away. Come on. I'll get us some food!"

I couldn't help but chuckle at him.

"Okay, since you woke up to kick the rooster and woke me up, I'll go. Only if we can have a picnic." I stood up and stretched as he cheered on the other end.

"All right! Be there in thirty." Eli hung up, and I stumbled to the kitchen, wondering how much coffee he had had today.

I soon found myself sitting in his passenger seat as he ordered from the drive-through.

"Do you want anything else?" He glanced over, and I shrugged.

"Did you get the drinks and the extra fries?" I started laughing as he relayed my words to the speaker.

"So," Eli spoke, driving along, "do you regret waking up?"

I rolled my eyes, digging through the bag. "No." I laughed as I started eating my fries.

"Exactly!" Eli laughed, and shortly we pulled into a park.

The blue sky was lightly decorated with thinning white clouds, and the sun warmed the green grass. Eli grabbed a blanket from the back as I gathered the food.

"I appreciate you doing this." I broke the silence as we walked toward a sunny spot.

"I know you've been needing this for a while." Eli spread the blanket over the cold ground, and I started to set the bags down.

Kids shrieked a way off as they raced to the playground. Two little robins soared over our heads and landed in a nearby maple. The sky was the bluest I'd seen in a while, and for once I felt, well, alive.

"Why is this working?" I saw Eli look at me out of the corner of my eye. "Every day, I push myself out of bed, drag myself to work, then go home and waste my day until I have to go to bed. Then when it's my off days, I'm in bed until noon, I grab some food, and then hate myself because I'm lazy. Why is just going outside and eating breakfast with a friend helping?"

Eli took a bite of his sandwich and looked at the scenery before us. He sipped his drink before he responded.

"I don't know. Nowadays, laziness and depression symptoms are so similar, it's so hard to tell. Burnout is hard to deal with, especially when it's the same routine every day. We all talk about taking care of ourselves, but when we think we're doing that, it just turns out to be basic survival."

I looked at him, and he finally made eye contact.

"It's okay to lie in bed and do nothing," he started, "but you've got to make sure you counteract it too. And if you need something like an accountability buddy, I'm right here."

I smiled and leaned in to give him a hug.

"Thank you."

"Anytime, anytime." He pulled back and looked at me. "Now is it okay if I eat your fries?"

Glass

Being vulnerable will break your heart
And being kind will tear you apart
You think they'll be honest, and they'll agree
But most just like spilling the tea

I heard my door creak open, and there stood a silhouetted Tate.

"Good, it's you!" I exclaimed. "Come here. I need to discuss something with you."

Tate eyed my room as he slowly let himself in. He was still professional and kept his guard up, even if it was just us.

I sat cross-legged on my bed as papers scattered around me. I shuffled through a couple before I spoke.

"So with everything going on and all, I wanted to get everyone a little something. All of my bodyguards and my cleaning crew have done so well that I just want them to enjoy their own families and spend time with them."

"That's very kind of you, but who will cover their shifts while they're out?" Tate asked, walking closer to my bed.

"Exactly what I'm worried about. I can't ask y'all to work extra. Y'all are already doing too much. So I thought about holding a party for everyone to enjoy with their families, but I'm truly lost on what to do. I was hoping to ask you for your opinion." I looked up as his usually straight face held confusion in it.

"Me?" Tate picked up a couple of my papers and glanced through them. "Ma'am, may I ask why you're asking me?"

"Please, call me Cassie. I'm asking you because I'm the closest to you and Alyssa, and she's been cleaning up the downstairs since 2:00 p.m. today. I figured you would know what the others would want." I stood up and stretched.

Tate chuckled and shook his head. "Ma'am, I know the majority of them would love the extra time with family, but there's a few that would still be alone with the extra time off."

I glanced and watched as he put down the papers and looked around the room.

"Where's your family at?" I started walking toward him as he looked up at me.

"My family is quite scattered around, honestly. My mother's in a nursing home. She's getting better care than what I could provide her." He sighed, and I placed my hand on his arm.

He jerked his arm, but only for him to let me leave my hand there.

"I'm sorry." I looked up at him as he made hollow eye contact.

"It's all right, ma'am." I shot him a look, and he shook his head. "All right, Cassie."

"So what would you want?" I stared at him inquisitively.

"That's a very unprofessional question, ma'am." He chuckled, and I shook my head.

"I'm being serious"—I laughed—"but honestly, what would you want?"

He turned to face me, and his hazel eyes were dark. I'm pretty sure I've never noticed them that dark before. Soon he was a half step closer, and my heart was a half beat quicker.

"Ma'am." His breaths were struggling. "If you don't find what I'm asking you offensive, may I ask to kiss you?"

Memories

Everything in a small town has memories
No matter how bad we wanna erase it
Each road, parking lot, and building has a story to tell
And that never fails

Click

People click after finding the human that works
It's weird being with someone helps through the hurt
Their love is pure and honest too
And they can't stand harming you
They try to prevent any wrong your way
They wanna be there to save the day
They're so unique you wonder why you didn't meet them before
Then you remember pounding on God's closed door
You wanted to complete the level before you were there
You even tried some cheat codes you had spare
But that ruined the game
Made it mess up
Love's not that way
But when it's before you know yourself
It sure feels like it does

Actually In Love

You love the way her eyes light up and how gentle her sweet voice
    sounds
Boy, you see everything in her, and you love it when the lights go out
The way she brightens up your day
Any ol' gray cloud turns into a sunny day
She gives you everything I've ever heard you say
Just imagine what it's like when she's actually in love

Internet

Don't tell me it gets easier
When back then, you would've hated the same line
All I want is a little sympathy
But I hear it every time

We're just a click away
From all the wrong things
Claiming that we hit the wrong thing
Then why does it happen all the time

Some people claim to be in love
But they constantly throw it away and pick it back up
For some quick-time fun

We beg for an old-time romance
And blame it on everything else
And we don't take responsibility
For the actions, we don't want our next generation to face for themselves

Tea

Just because you talk to listening ears doesn't mean they have understanding souls

Just because you talk in a safe place doesn't mean they'll make it stay secretive and alone

People talk to have something to do

Some have done it to me as it was done to you

It's interesting to hear tea that's freshly brewed

But what happens when it's spilled amongst others too?

The pure white carpet has a blotchy brown sticky stain

While others stare and walk away

It's not their mess

They don't have to clean it up

And you're left with tracks of mud

Some have hearts of genuine and pure gold

While others it takes a while to see that it's cold

We can both be gorgeous
One's beauty is not another's lack of

—Lexxie Barner

Endings

Just because that's where it ended in the movie doesn't
mean that's where your life stops at too.

Someone contacting you for what you can offer doesn't define your value. It defines how they choose to see others.

Candle

She looks in the mirror but doesn't see
The looks and person you love to watch her be
She's been told the good things multiple times
And she's heard the bad enough to make her cry
She makes herself cry as her mind tears apart her own skin
All she wants is to feel whole again
She's unsure how to love the woman she sees
When all she knows is the girl chained with anxiety
She doesn't see her eyes light up with joy
She doesn't see her face as she's prideful for her boy
She likes stuff about herself
Don't get her wrong
But sometimes the bad makes all the good long gone
She wants to love herself all the time
But all we've been taught is to idolize
She loves herself
Less than what she should
But once she finally sees herself
Watch her light up the whole room

Prefer

There's a lot of dos and a lot of don'ts
And people will always tell you which ones you want
There's a lot of truths and a lot of lies
And each one will get you every time
There's a lot of confusion going on
But apparently everyone else but themselves are wrong, so just move on
There's a lot to be unsure about
And none of us are sure how it goes down
There's a lot of choices for your life you can make
But the wrong one will automatically make you a disgrace
There's a lot of different views in this world
But it doesn't matter
Are you sure that you're heard
You have a voice
When you say something they like
It doesn't matter
We're all biased inside

Somebody's Baby

Just listen, okay? That's someone's baby. You may not agree, like, get along, think, believe, and act like them, and that's okay. Just please, respect and love them like you want to be loved and respected.

Thank You

I just want to say thank you to everyone who's currently been in or out of my life. Thank you to the people who are by my side right now and those who can't be. You've done so much for me, and I love you all greatly for it. I want you to know that you all mean so much to me, and I couldn't be here without you.

Thank you for the inspiration, the advice, and for being there. I appreciate every moment as I hope you do when you read this book.

With much love and prayers, I'm only a phone call away.

—Sarah Dill